G000123790

This book provides a simple method for foretelling the future - a method that anyone can use. The runes, an esoteric system of divination and prediction, have been known for thousands of years. The conventional set of runes consists of 24 symbols, each one with a particular meaning, engraved on a piece of bone, wood or stone (or printed on cards nowadays). The runes have magical significance, and today, they are a popular method of predicting the future - a prediction that you can make for yourself. This book will teach you about each rune and its interpretation, and how to use the runes for your own benefit. The book is richly illustrated.

Hali Morag was born to a family of Hungarian origin, in which mysticism, including Tarot cards, dream interpretation and so on, played an important role. He writes books on various aspects of mysticism, and divides his time between Israel, India and France.

LITTLE **BIG** BOOK

of

Runes

by Hali Morag

Astrolog Publishing House

ᚠ
ᚢ
ᚦ
ᚹ
ᛗ
ᚷ
ᛒ

Astrolog Publishing House
P.O. Box 1123, Hod Hasharon 45111, Israel
Tel: 972-9-7412044
Fax: 972-9-7442714
E-Mail: info@astrolog.co.il
Astrolog Web Site: www.astrolog.co.il

© Hali Morag 1999

ISBN 965-494-038-8

All rights reserved. No part of this publication may be
reproduced, stored in a retrieval system, or transmitted in
any form or by any means, electronic, mechanical,
photocopying, recording or otherwise, without the prior
permission of the publisher.

Published by Astrolog Publishing House 1999

Printed in Israel
10 9 8 7 6 5 4 3 2 1

INTRODUCTION

The runes, in the form of stones or cards, constitute a method of prediction which began millennia ago. Researchers claim that the method originated in Phoenicia, and it is clear that the various symbols closely resemble the characters of ancient Phoenician script.

In a manner which is unknown to us today, the rune method reached Northern Europe, where it was closely guarded by the Scandinavian peoples until the sixteenth century. The runes penetrated central Europe during the Renaissance, and, in parallel with Tarot cards, became a popular method of predicting the future.

The runes are, in fact, 24 cards, each containing a different symbol. There is a 25th card which is blank (similar to the Joker). Every card has a name and meaning. In this book, the names and accepted "Scandinavian" nicknames of the cards are listed. Some cards have different meanings - upright and reverse, according to the direction in which the card pointed when it was extracted. Other cards have only one meaning, and they are easily identifiable since the character that appears on them looks the same, no matter which way it faced when it was taken out of the pack.

A calendar in which the runes indicate the future.

The runes, in the form of cards, stones (similar to domino pieces) upon which the symbols were engraved, or special coins, were used mainly for predicting the future. The interpreter would make a prediction for himself or for others by shuffling the pack and extracting a number of cards, as is done with playing cards.

In recent years, there has been a turnabout in the use of the runes. They are now used in the West on a far more personal level, and are more closely connected to awareness than to the prediction of actual events.

Many people have a pack of rune cards or stones, and extract, for example, three every morning. The first rune predicts what will happen in the morning, the second gives a forecast of the afternoon's events, and the third foretells what the evening holds. It is customary to write down the various interpretations of the runes in a diary, and to refer to them at the end of the day to see whether the predictions were accurate. This is how a "Rune Diary" is kept in the West.

The runes closely resemble the I Ching. In both cases, the prediction and the analysis are performed in an intuitive manner. When a particular rune is chosen, there are several sentences, properties or associations connected with it.

The rune does not always provide a direct answer to our question or problem, but it can indicate a general direction or tendency. After the rune has been extracted, the interpreter has to create a bridge between the rune and the interpretation.

ᚠ
ᚢ
ᛈ
ᛗ
ᛒ

A bracelet containing rune symbols, used as an amulet.

In recent years, researchers have begun to expose many methods of prediction and of character analysis that resemble the runes. One of them is the I Ching, and similar methods have been found in ancient Inca culture (ropes and knots in different colors), the High Priest's breastplate in Judaism, and so on.

It transpires that the runes exerted an influence on many methods for predicting the future. We find their influence not only in various mystical realms, but also in styles of building (mainly in the construction of churches and temples), in writing tablets, and in various symbols and amulets.

While the aim of this book is not to delve into the fascinating phenomenon of the runes in great detail or depth, the reader will certainly be given the foundations of the method.

A list of the 25 runes and their descriptions (including the reverse position) is presented here, together with an illustration of each one. After the descriptions, a number of methods for opening the runes or interpreting them in a spread are proposed.

The runes afford an excellent daily oracle for helping a person discern the path he should take and the fate that awaits him.

The interpretation of the runes is valid for runes both in upright and reverse position: If its base faces the querent, it is in upright position. Some of the runes have symbols which look the same whether the rune is in upright or reverse position, and they are only interpreted in one way - upright. See, for example, page 56.

1. MANNAZ
The Self: Man, the individual or the human race.

According to the mannaz rune, the beginning of everything is in the self, and the source is found in clear water. The connection between the self and the rest of creation comes about by means of water.

The mannaz rune reflects a person's attitude toward others and their attitude toward the person. In other words, it deals with friends and foes.

Modesty is an expression of the self. Be modest. Try to adopt a life of modesty as your path, a path where there is also pride and honor.

This is the time to prepare the greatness which is awaiting you in your future. This is the time to plow the field in readiness for sowing.

Do the things you have to do for the sake of the doing and not for the sake of the result. This is the way to become experienced with the reality that is behind the veil.

The mannaz rune contains the wunjo rune (Joy), since happiness is found in the self.

Know yourself! It is a gift.

ᚠ
ᚢ
ᚦ
ᛗ
ᛒ

Reverse

When there is an obstacle, a blockage, do not turn to others. Seek the solution within yourself. You are your own worst enemy. When you see what you reflect around you, you can find and identify your inner enemy.

Remember: From the point of view of your body, you are young, mature or old. From the point of view of your soul, you are but an infant!

ᚠ
ᚢ
ᚦ
ᛗ
ᛒ

2. GEBO

Partnership: A gift, a sacrifice, offerings from the gods or from chiefs to loyal followers.

Everything exists in partnership, and a partnership of any kind (members of a couple, a business partnership, a team working toward a specific goal, and so on) is on the horizon. The gebo rune signifies exchanges, contracts and personal relationships.

True partnership can be achieved only when the self (mannaz) exhausts its uniqueness and invests it in the renewed union.

True partnership always gives the spirit leeway to gather around every individual. But it must be remembered that the strength of every partnership is like the strength of the connection between its members.

The partnership of the self is the perfect partnership between the person and his Self: body, soul and spirit.

The gebo rune relates to gifts in two ways: giving from generosity, and giving as a sacrifice.

ᚠ

ᚢ

ᚦ

ᛗ

ᛒ

Reverse

The gebo rune has no reverse, and it can therefore work according to the "four winds of Heaven" in every situation.

ᚠ
ᚢ
ᚦ
ᛗ
ᛒ

3. ANSUZ
Signals: Blessings, especially in a religious context; the consolation provided by faith.

The ansuz rune - signals - is the artery of life, of life itself. Signals are an indication of receiving messages, knowledge and feelings. The very nature of runes is to bring messages of supreme truth, and this is where the importance of the ansuz rune lies.

The ansuz rune is the spark that initiates new contacts and new beginnings. It opens up the new paths.

The ansuz rune is the expression of the god Loki (the Nordic messenger god). When this rune is revealed, it means that something new is about to begin.

Signals are a prerequisite for any change, whether it concerns one rune only, or a spread consisting of several runes.

Signals are also a reminder. When you receive a signal, you must not forget to add a little of yourself to it, that is, to the meaning of the signals.

Reverse

Difficulties in communication (reception problems), a lack of awareness of the true situation. A feeling of a lack of productivity. A need for consultation or advice. Possible retreat.

4. OTHILA
Separation: Property, inheritance - financial, spiritual, experiential and value-based.

A fork in the road, a crossroads, where the old is left behind and the new lies ahead. Examine the way of retreat and plan the path ahead.

Separation occurs (how sad!) mainly in the material realm: inheritance, the disposition of property, the sale of property. Only after he detaches himself from the past, from his roots, does man discover their true value; thus detachment becomes separation.

There has to be a test or growth of free will in separation. Man is now supposed to rely only upon himself, and not on other people or things. This retreat is necessary for attack.

Reverse
This is not the time to remain in the past or rely on it. During this process, it is important to think of and remember not only the Self, but also others. Absolute honesty is required (and not always found). Remember that although we participate completely passively in the course of

creation, it is always preferable for us to add something of our own.

5. URUZ
Strength: Physical strength and speed; a sacrificial animal, the Aurochs.*

The uruz rune makes new beginnings possible, and allows man to live the kind of life that is right for him. It bestows upon man the power of the legendary phoenix to rise from the ashes and begin over again.

Change comes from the ashes. Man therefore requires strength in order to extract light from the darkness. His life contains many transitions: death, birth, fertility, growth, fading, rebirth, and so on, and strength enables him to emerge fortified from each one.

The uruz rune makes the unification of the soul with the universe possible, so as to bring about new growth. This is masculinity. This is femininity. This is untamed nature.

Reverse

When a person has no ears, he cannot hear; when he has no eyes, he cannot see. This rune, in reverse, demands that he carefully consider the structure of his Self. Remember that in darkness,

*(a now extinct species of wild cattle)

in the absence of light, he learns to grope his way. Without a boat, he learns to swim.

ᚠ
ᚢ
ᚦ
ᛗ
ᛒ

6. PERTHO
Initiation: The meaning is uncertain, mysterious.

Initiation signifies the mystery that transcends man's understanding. It is the hidden, the source of the fire that sparks life. It is a deep secret. pertho concerns female matters and mysteries, including fertility. It represents creativity waiting to materialize.

Initiation is the change beneath the surface, and the secret of this change is well hidden; only a few chosen ones are privy to it.

Initiation is the path to understanding Fate; **it** resembles the eagle which hovers above the soul, seeing and examining everything.

Although initiation is external, it is expressed only in the internal part of man, in his soul and spirit. Therefore, the pertho rune enables the spirit to be renewed and the soul to be purified, and its source is in the mystery of life.

Reverse
Be careful that your level of aspirations and expectations does not exceed what is possible for you. There is no way back. Concentrate your efforts, since initiation demands that you "cut

short" the present in order to ensure the future.

Always see the glass as half full rather than half empty. In this way, you will be able to overcome the difficulties of initiation.

ᚠ
ᚢ
ᚦ
ᛗ
ᛒ

7. NAUTHIZ
Constraint: Need, necessity, restriction, human suffering and sorrow, lessons.

Constraint is need. Constraint is pain. Constraint is something that man imposes on himself. Constraint is something that the environment imposes on man.

The nauthiz rune identifies the realm of constraint, the "shadow" that it casts on man's life and actions. The main lesson that nauthiz teaches is: "Don't take it personally!" Identify the constraint, set the situation right, but do not consider every "shadow" as a plot against you personally.

Constraint testifies to difficulties and obstacles along your path, but it also teaches that you are capable of surmounting them. By means of good will, sorrow will be averted in the future. Turn back. Examine your mistakes. Pay the price for them. Mend your ways. Consider, think and consult. Hard work will bring relief from the suffering caused by financial constraints.

Reverse
The nauthiz rune, which appears after the pertho rune, teaches the essence of pain, failure

and the constraint of the self. Even at moments of shining light, at the pinnacle of glory, the shadow can darken the scene.

Only the light in the Self will enable us to see the strength that resides in us, so that we can pave our way. Suffering leads to understanding. Darkness leads to light. Remain composed and be of good disposition.

8. INGUZ
Fertility: Male fertility, matters of health, family and offspring. Ing, the legendary hero, who later became a god.

Fertility is a new beginning. The inguz rune is, therefore, the reflection of the moon, directing us to the intuitive in us, to harmony and wholeness (especially in our personal relationships).

Seek what is similar.

We always find joy and happiness in a new beginning, in a new path. When the inguz rune is cast, you have the strength and power for a new beginning.

For the plant to grow, the seed must be planted, watered, hoed and given fertilizer. In order to do this, a great deal of effort must be put into the new beginning. The old remains behind. The new paves its way, coming and rising from the old.

The inguz rune will occasionally direct you to liberate yourself from former habits and to adopt a new way of life. Always remember: The new is based on the old!

Movement is dangerous. Stagnation is the end of the line.

ᚠ
ᚾ
ᚹ
ᛗ
ᛒ

Free yourself of the bonds that bind you to the earth. Raise your eyes to the infinite heavens.

Reverse
The very nature of fertility means that it has no reverse (since it always goes forward).

9. EIHWAZ
Defense: Yew tree, a bow made of yew wood, rune magic, avertive powers, the driving force to acquire.

The meaning of defense is overcoming obstacles. Every obstacle that is surmounted is by definition a step forward.

When defense leads to an obstacle in man's soul (that is, when tension, anxiety and nervousness occur), this is very bad. When defense is carried out with logic, patience and tolerance, and the path is clear, this is very good. This is how the eihwaz rune works: "The obstacle has been removed and the path ahead is clear."

The eihwaz rune demands patience, in the form of a delay. Therefore the meaning of defense is also "a period of ripening" before the deed, especially when the obstacle manifests itself as a task or a new path.

When we know how to decide, we know how to do. The eihwaz rune motivates us and gives us a sense of purpose.

The eihwaz rune warns against difficulties, but promises success. "By the sweat of your brow you will succeed."

Know your path, and you will be able to go along it.

Reverse

The eihwaz rune has no reverse, since it reverses things itself (that is, it eliminates the obstacle in front of it).

ᚠ
ᚢ
ᚦ
ᛗ
ᛒ

10. ALGIZ
Protection: Defense, the urge to shelter or protect oneself and others, maintaining hard-earned success; the elk, sedge.

Protection is safeguarding the status of the Self. In times of transition, of change, of crisis, there is a tendency to become addicted to emotions. This addiction can be a fall as well as a rise. The algiz rune gives us the strength to be ourselves in every situation.

For man, protection is like spiritual intoxication, which enables him to safeguard his Self even when events and extraneous influences attempt to change him.

Protection enables man to have feelings and experiences, even painful ones, without disconnecting from himself.

Progress instead of disconnecting!

Follow your path; that is the best protection of all.

Reverse

If too much pressure is exerted on the Self, that is, heavy and persistent external pressures on the protective armor - it is liable to be harmful to physical and emotional health.

Do not let others take advantage of you!

Safeguarding the status of your Self will prevent exploitation.

If you safeguard your position, you may not win, but you will not lose either!

ᚠ

ᚢ

ᚹ

ᛗ

ᛒ

11. FEHU

Possessions: Present or future financial strength and prosperity, property, possessions earned or won.

Possessions are the realization of aspirations, they are love, they are material and spiritual reward. Man's reward on earth is a reflection of how his deeds are seen in heaven.

Possessions create the correct balance between a desire and its realization, between what is desired and what actually exists.

The fehu rune is important principally during a period of success, as it prevents the abuse of success. Learn to take advantage of success and good luck; this is just as important as fighting bad luck!

Reverse

When the fehu rune comes up in reverse, you can expect disappointments in many areas of life. You will not succeed in attaining all of your objectives and in realizing all of your aspirations.

Scrutinize yourself thoroughly and determine what you have to do in order to reform yourself and change your life.

Do not be tempted by groundless festivities,

nor be carried away by chance success; however, you should not sink into despair either!

Remember that when the fehu rune is in reverse, its shadow falls on you; while you are in its shadow, you will not fulfill yourself.

ᚠ
ᚢ
ᚦ
ᛗ
ᛒ

12. WUNJO

Joy: Pleasure - even a surfeit of pleasure. In moderation, it means success and acknowledgment of worth, the absence of suffering and sorrow.

Joy is light. When the wunjo rune is cast, the tree bears fruit. A period of searching for the way comes to an end, and the time has come to receive the blessing of joy - the joy of life, of doing, of sex. Joy brings a period of happiness, in which man fulfills himself, and, even more importantly, feels satisfaction with this fulfillment.

Joy brings happiness back into man's life - not happiness that stems from the material or the intellectual, but basic happiness that comes from emotions. Joy is the first step to light, to God, to the Supreme. Joy brings new energy into man's life, dissipates the clouds and the darkness, and colors everything in the bright color of light. Joy is like the sun which rises in the East, and opens a window to a new life. The wunjo rune shows the way to the pure Self.

Reverse
The fruit does not ripen, the shoot does not

grow. Rebirth is being delayed, and suddenly there is a growing fear of the new and of change. There is a barrier which impedes joy, a barrier that exists within yourself - the barrier of foolishness, of stupidity, of indifference. Eliminate the barrier and the flow of things will resume. The wunjo rune reminds man that he is always being tested. In difficult times, wunjo in reverse reminds man to muster his emotional powers in preparation for trials and struggles.

13. JERA
Harvest: A fruitful year. Hopes of peace, prosperity and success. Rewards for previous efforts.

The jera rune testifies to positive results - but it must be remembered that there is a time lapse between the rune and the result. The jera rune relates to the harvest, the cycle of seasons, and it transpires that the harvest - the result - reaches fruition within one year.

He who sows will reap. But from the time of sowing to the time of reaping, there is a period when the crops must be watered, given fertilizer, weeded, trimmed, cared for and nurtured. Sowing alone is insufficient.

The result depends not only on the seed, but also on the care it receives.

The key word for the jera rune is patience. Its natural and positive course cannot be accelerated for fear of jeopardizing the process of reaching fruition!

Reverse
The jera rune has no reverse, as the ruin of the harvest results from a lack of care, or from

incorrect care, during the interval between the rune and the result.

ᚠ
ᚢ
ᚦ
ᛗ
ᛒ

14. KAUNAZ
Opening: Torch, ulcer, possibly a warning of health problems, both mental and physical.

Opening is fire.
Opening is a torch.
Opening is renewal.
Opening brings light and dispels darkness.
Opening indicates the path to a renewed relationship.
Opening that appears in the morning (that is, as the first rune in the series of three - morning, noon and evening), testifies to a successful day.
The kaunaz rune is an especially positive rune when it appears at the beginning of a spread of the runes.
A spread opens the consciousness so that it can absorb the Supreme Light.

Reverse
The kaunaz rune in reverse indicates weakening and a process of diminishing. Whatever was good before will be less good now. Whatever was bad before will be truly terrible now.
Personal relationships will be damaged.

The path you are taking is not the right one. The kaunaz rune in reverse signifies that you must change your path.

The kaunaz rune (reversed) is a serious warning sign.

15. TEIWAZ

Warrior: Honor, justice, authority, victory in battle, a guiding star, success in general and in legal affairs.

The warrior is not a warrior whose strength lies in the realms of the material or the soul, but rather in the spiritual. He is the spiritual warrior, and spiritual warfare takes place within a person. The teiwaz rune causes you to become aware of where your true strengths lie. It directs you to look inward, deep down within yourself. Only with this internal gaze can you understand your vocation and realize it.

It is important to understand that the warrior is a rune that is also associated with action, and is therefore linked to the sun. However, it must be remembered that it is not a question of war and external conquest, but of self-conquest. The way of the warrior is the awareness of the Self, the identification of the vocation of the Self and its realization.

The warrior is the one who has the courage to remove the internal veil and see the Self with eyes wide open. The warrior stands beside you in the war between the Self and temptation, so, in other words, a warrior is one who can overcome his temptation.

Reverse

The kaunaz rune in reverse testifies that the forces and routine of life were what swept you away, making you stray from the right path. Examine the motives for your actions and look for the right path. Remember that the path exists inside you.

It is easy to ignore the spiritual warrior inside you; it is much more difficult to eliminate the consequences of the wrong path.

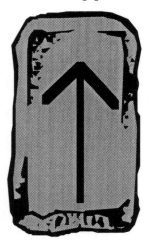

16. BERKANA
Growth: General fertility - physical, mental and econonic, fertility cults, rebirth, new life, personal growth.

Growth is rebirth.

The berkana rune, which is cyclical, relates to the cycle of fertility - either symbolic or physical. Growth (by means of fertility) can express itself either in an increase in awareness and enlightenment, or in physical growth and development.

Growth is the flow in which the essence passes from one form to another, revealing a flow of changes. The smoother the current, the more stable and calm it is. When there are obstacles, the flow overcomes them, but creates a whirlpool in so doing. The importance of growth, therefore, does not lie only in the current, but also in the obstacles over which it flows.

When the flow, or growth, is stable, it ultimately eliminates the obstacle and smoothes out the path ahead.

Reverse
The obstacles are serious, they divert the flow from its path, block it, and create whirlpools and

ᚠ
ᚢ
ᚦ
ᛗ
ᚱ

waterfalls. Sometimes the obstacle absorbs the current and turns it into a foul pool of stagnant water. The first stage is to identify the obstacle; only then can it be removed.

ᚠ
ᚢ
ᚦ
ᛗ
ᛒ

17. EHWAZ
Movement: A message from the gods; confirms the surrounding runes; associated with the course of the sun.

Progress is movement. Movement is progress.

Movement - whether it is physical movement from place to place, whether it is movement from one standpoint to another in life, whether it is movement to improve your situation - physical, spiritual or emotional.

The ehwaz rune can indicate slow, stable, fixed movement, but occasionally the movement is in leaps, when there is a period of calm between fast movements.

Movement relates to the individual, to an idea, to an enterprise - in fact, to everything that exists in the world.

The ehwaz rune does what was said previously: You will reap what you have sowed. (In many places, this rune is identified with the horse, which affords safe and rapid movement forward. This belief is a residue of the rune techniques used in the Middle Ages.)

Reverse
Movement that encounters a barrier. Not

every open path attracts you, and not every possibility is really feasible. Level-headedness is more important than a leap forward.

ᚠ
ᚢ
ᚦ
ᛗ
ᚱ

18. LAGUZ
Flow: Water, sea, a source of fertility; success in travel or acquisition, but also possible loss.

Flow is water which is changing its place.

Water has no apparent inherent strength. Even an infant can put his hand into the ocean and "hurt" it or "kick" it.

However, water is also the strongest force in the world: It has the power to sweep away, to erode and to change whatever stands in its path.

This is the laguz rune. This rune is important especially concerning the flow of consciousness, the influence of the subconscious and the moon (the tides are determined by the phases of the moon). Some people go so far as to say that the moon is the ruler of the flow, while the sun is its barrier.

The laguz rune marks the time which is appropriate for initiation, for development, for clearing the mind, for reorganization. It relates mainly to spiritual awareness, and much less to the physical or the behavioral.

Reverse
A warning sign: You are relying on the material in your life, and you are not taking your

intuition or your subconscious wisdom into account.

ᚠ
ᚢ
ᚦ
ᛗ
ᛒ

19. HAGALAZ
Disruption: Hail, sleet; harmful, uncontrolled natural forces, both in the physical and the unconscious realms, as well as in the weather.

Chaos is disruption - but the entire world was created from chaos!

The hagalaz rune is extremely important as it relates to change, liberty, the ability to initiate and invent, and freedom from the bonds of thought. The rune testifies to an urgent need to escape the bonds and act in the correct way.

It is important to emphasize that especially in this rune, its reverse interpretation is the same as its upright. It has a lot of strength, and its appearance in a spread or in a casting demands profound consideration.

This is a warning sign - something will go wrong in your life if you do not perform a certain action.

This rune can indicate a need for simple and easy action, or a significant and essential need in a person's life.

20. RAIDO
Journey: Travel - both physical and through life; the soul after death.

In olden times, the physical journey from place to place constituted the main and only means of communication. Moreover, every journey involved a detachment (from the place of origin) and a union (with the destination), a detachment (from the destination) and a reunion (with the place of origin).

A journey is a process of communication, involving union and detachment, either between a person and other people, or between a person and himself. A journey can be to the depths of the soul, to the subconscious, to enlightenment - or to the top of Mount Everest!

A journey is the means to self-change, to self-healing, to the union of the person with himself. It is deciding upon the right move to make. But this journey must originate from inside the person himself, and of his own free will - and never because of constraints.

Reverse
Difficulties in the "journey processes" (that

is, in creating communication) with others and with yourself.

ᚠ
ᚢ
ᚦ
ᛗ
ᚱ

21. THURISAZ
Gateway: Giant, demon, thorn, aggressive conflicts and complications, unreliability.

The gateway is the place where the internal meets the external, the conscious meets the subconscious, the open meets the concealed, the heavens meet the earth.

The gateway, in order to be a gateway, generally requires that someone pass through it. This is not the case here. The thurisaz rune demands that you stop and stand motionless, doing nothing. **Wait!** This rune gives you the strength to wait. There is no need to do anything. There is no need to decide.

The thurisaz rune provides you with the possibility of stopping and consolidating yourself and your path. You do not have to walk and pass through it. When you are ready, you will find yourself **passing through the gateway**, without any action on your part.

Reverse
You are acting in haste. You have the opportunity to stop and consider, but you tend to miss this opportunity.

22. DAGAZ

Breakthrough: Day, prosperity and fruitfulness, security and certainty; the clarity of daylight as opposed to the uncertainty of night-time.

Breakthrough is metamorphosis.

This rune, when it concludes a process (especially a process of study or initiation) is extremely important. Breakthrough symbolizes metamorphosis, like a caterpillar turns into a butterfly. Sometimes, metamorphosis can be extreme, and sometimes it is almost indiscernible.

Breakthrough at the right time is the secret of success. A time for all things. A time to plan an enterprise, or to embark upon one.

Metamorphosis at the inappropriate time (or in the wrong direction) is not effective. A butterfly does not turn into a caterpillar!

Metamorphosis - be it from the material to the spiritual, from evil to good - is best if it happens at the end of the process.

There is no reverse here, since metamorphosis is dependent on the process of after/before.

ᚠ
ᚢ
ᚦ
ᛉ
ᚦ

23. ISA
Standstill: Ice, freezing, psychological blocks to thought or activity.

Standstill is water which has frozen.

The isa rune testifies that "cold" (or winter) has descended upon man. Darkness descended upon day. But you must remember that this period can be either good or bad: good when the standstill is exploited for a "rebirth", bad when the standstill becomes a fixed thing.

Isa is a rune which reinforces the meanings of those around it. It also demands dealing with the Self. When everything is flowing, everyone participates in the process. When standstill takes over, you are alone, only with yourself.

The isa rune has no reverse.

ᚠ
ᚢ
ᚦ
ᛗ
ᚱ

ᚠ
ᚢ
ᚦ
ᛉ
ᚱ

24. SOWULO

**Wholeness: The sun, the life-force; good health
or other good circumstances; harmony in the
future.**

Wholeness is the aim of every person.
Wholeness is the life-force. Wholeness is the
circular sun.

The quest for wholeness is the way of the
spiritual warrior. This rune has tremendous
power. Although it has no reverse, it obliges man
to be cautious, since wholeness is not granted - it
is acquired.

Wholeness is the aim, the way and the means.
Remember that!

THE UNKNOWABLE:
A blank rune which can be white or black.

This is the end. This is the beginning. This is the birth. This is the death. This is up. This is down.

Remember: Self-change is your life path!

(This rune is not counted as one of the regular runes. Some people recommend ignoring it completely, and taking it out of the pack.)

ᚠ
ᚢ
ᚦ
ᛗ
ᚱ

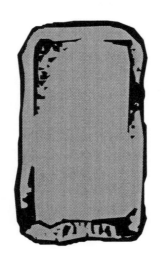

Spreads of the Runes

The single-rune method

A wonderfully simple and effective method. Every time a problem or question crops up, the runes are cast, one rune is selected, and the interpretation is made accordingly. This method should not be used more than two or three times a day.

ᚠ

ᚢ

ᚹ

ᛗ

ᚱ

The three-rune method

Three runes are selected and laid down. The one on the left represents morning, the middle one represents noon, and the one on the right represents evening.

This method should be used once a day, every day - using the same method of choosing the three runes in this spread.

Morning   Noon   Evening

ᚠ
ᚢ
ᚦ
ᛗ
ᚱ

The seven-rune method

Seven runes are selected and are placed vertically, one beneath the other (see diagram). The top one is Monday, the next Tuesday, and so on, up till the rune which is Sunday. (It does not matter when the spread is done - the prediction always begins from the following Monday!)

Monday

Sunday

F
Π
P
M
B

The whole rune spread

The whole rune spread utilizes 13 different runes. This is the largest of the rune spreads, and for that reason is called the "whole rune spread". (The number of unused runes will not suffice to produce another whole rune spread.)

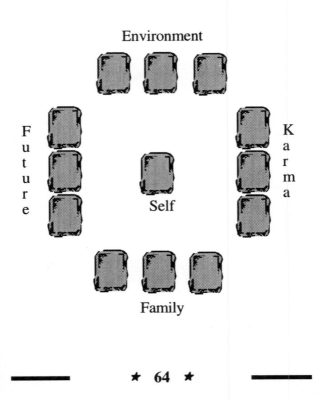

ᚠ
ᚢ
ᚦ
ᛗ
ᛒ

The first rune, placed in the middle, is the **Self** rune, that is, it relates to the querent [the person who is asking the question] - who he is and what his character is.

The top row reflects the **environment** in which the person lives: the society, the country, his workplace, and so on.

The bottom row reflects the person's **family**, whether his family of origin or his present family.

The left column teaches us about the **future** and **fate** of the person.

The right column teaches us about the **karma** - what the person brought with him as a birth inheritance, or as his reincarnation.

The middle rune is interpreted by itself. The rows and columns are interpreted by means of a combination of the meanings of the three different runes.

ᚠ
ᚢ
ᚦ
ᛗ
ᚱ

The weekly diary

A popular, effective and flexible use of the runes is keeping a weekly diary.

To use this method - which is easy for everybody - you need a diary in which all the days of the week appear on one page or on a double-page spread.

[At this point, we will remark that the reverse position can be ignored in this method: All the runes can be considered "upright".]

At a fixed time each morning, one rune is selected from the pack, and its name is written on the first line of the diary for the particular day.

Then the interpretation of the rune is examined, and a short sentence is written under the name of the rune. This sentence expresses the person's feeling concerning the question, "How will this day be for me?"

For instance, the person takes out rune number 23 - isa (Standstill). He feels that this rune predicts a "rebirth", and he writes the sentence: "Despite the difficulties, I believe that today I will succeed in solving the tough problem I am facing, and I will begin to go along a new and better path."

At the end of the day, the person must return to his diary, look at the sentence he wrote, and decide for himself whether the prediction he made that morning has come true.

The person writes his conclusion under the first sentence.

For instance: "Although I tried, in all honesty, to solve the problem, the other party did not cooperate, and the whole situation is in an unresolvable crisis at the moment."

It is important for the person to make sure that he selects one rune at the same fixed time each morning, and that he writes the sentence and the conclusion.

At the end of the week, he will have seven entries. Now, the entire week is related to as if it were one whole spread - the advantage being that we have the prediction and its realization! That is, we can test the predictive ability of the runes.

The person can distinguish, for example, that his forecast for each day (based on the daily rune) was excessively optimistic. Conclusion: His interpretation of the runes was too optimistic. The following week, in order to decrease the discrepancy, he can be more "pessimistic" in the formulation of his daily sentence.

In this way, the person learns to interpret and relate to the runes when the background to the interpretation is **his own life!** Moreover, the quality of his predictions improves with time. After a period of between five and eight weeks, he will discover that his predictive ability has improved astonishingly.

At the end of each month, the person should go over the four weeks and summarize his conclusions. This procedure is also recommended for the year.

When the person is facing a special event, he may select two runes from the pack. The first relates to the actual day, and the second to the important event.

An important and central stage in this use of the runes is inner contemplation, or meditation.

After the person has selected the rune and written the sentence, he must focus on what is written, "roll" it around his mind, and feel what is written. This inner contemplation is actually a preparation for the new day.

Similarly, the conclusion should be contemplated at the end of the day.

Keeping a personal rune diary is becoming popular and widespread, and people who use this method regularly report that there has been a significant improvement in their quality of life.

Example of one week in a rune diary

GEBO

Monday: I'm going on a blind date tonight. I hope something comes of it.

Nice guy, but not for me!

KAUNAZ

Tuesday: I really must confide in others more. Maybe I surround myself with too many defenses.

Lousy day! Someone smashed into my car while it was parked, and didn't leave a note.

EHWAZ

Wednesday: I must change something in my life. I must keep my eyes open and find new opportunities.

They've offered me a new position at work. I have to give them an answer by the end of the month.

Thursday: To change or not to change? I don't know what to do.

LAGUZ

The guy I went out with on Monday called. I rejected him.

Friday: What's the matter with me? Why can't I grab opportunities and try new things?

ISA

Lousy day. I fought with everyone.

Saturday: This is the second time I've picked this rune. Is it trying to tell me something?

GEBO

I've decided to accept the offer of the new position.

Sunday: I feel great! The change will help me.

RADIO

Met someone nice today. Maybe this was my week after all!

Weekly summary:

I see that during the week, my expectations were high, but so was my self-criticism. I must take life more easily. My expectations do me harm because they cause me unnecessary tension. Next week, I will try to be less optimistic. Don't forget - on Tuesday I start my new position. I have to remember to take out TWO runes in the morning.

ᚠ
ᚢ
ᚦ
ᛗ
ᚱ